Blackest Ever Hole

BLACKEST EVER HOLE

Brian O'Blivion

gnOme

BLACKEST EVER HOLE
© Brian O'Blivion and gnOme books

This work is licensed under the Creative Commons Attribution-NonCommerical-NoDerivs 3.0 Unported License. To view a copy of this license, visit: http://creativecommons.org/licenses/by-nc-nd/3.0.

gnomebooks.wordpress.com

Please address inquiries to:
gnOmebooks@gmail.com

ISBN-13: 978-0615752297 (gnOme)
ISBN-10: 0615752292

Cover image: Ernst Haeckel, *Kunstformen der Natur* (1904), plate 58, Tineida. Public domain image. Source: http://en.wikipedia.org/wiki/File:Haeckel_Tineida.jpg

Because it was a cold night, and the house was unheated, the smell was not terribly strong. I knelt at the edge of the hole and shone the flashlight into it as far as its thin beam would reach. But the only other objects I could see were some broken bottles stuck within the strata of human waste. I thought about what other things might be in that basement . . . and I became lost in those thoughts.

THOMAS LIGOTTI

CONTENTS

Introduction: Broadcast	8
PART ONE – GRAVITATIONAL COLLAPSE	
An Act of Kindness	11
Carnivore	16
Negative Pressure	17
Pinhead	18
The Nightmare Room	19
Inside the Black Box	20
Untitled	21
Cavity	22
My Brother's Head	23
My Father's Head	24
My Family Grave	25
Ghost Factory	26
Chasm	27
Death by a Thousand Cuts	28

Humiliation	29
Say Kill, Kill, Kill	30
Tyrant Unto Ruins	31

PART TWO – COAGULATION OF HOLES

Chamber Music	33
Inside Space	37
The Abyss	38
Stranger	39
Punching Clown	41
The Destruction Loops	46
Pluto	59
Death Manual: Instructions for Participation in a Mass Suicide Ritual	60
Below the Violet	61

PART THREE – EVAPORATION

Screwhead	67
Acknowledgements	73

INTRODUCTION

Broadcast

Brothers, 3 and 4, found dead in car

Yellowstone grizzly roams free after mauling

Scientists find first superbug strain of gonorrhea

Confirmed! Americans happier on weekends

Knife-wielding "soul collector" will plead guilty

Someone injuring cyclists with tacks

Robber beat up by hair salon owner and kept as sex slave

Woman cuts off husband's penis, tosses it in garbage disposal

Murder-castration tied to sex cult

Man writes identical sentence every day for entire year, commits suicide

Bear-safety lecture interrupted by bear

Woman runs over ex-boyfriend—twice—after he insults her mother

Body parts of missing 8-year-old boy found in dumpster

New restaurant is inside prison, staffed by inmates

3-year-old girl killed by mom's boyfriend for not eating at dinner time

Truck spills 14 million bees on highway

Girl found eating herself in cage in mobile home

What do women and dogs have in common? Neither allowed at golf club

No charges in amputee vet's roller coaster death

NASA satellite disappears in black hole, relays images of ourselves in nightmarish pancake makeup, staring

PART ONE

Gravitational Collapse

An Act of Kindness

You got towns where moss gets tossed around. And towns where wind fusses up dust in your mouth. We got rolling heads. We got heads that roll right up to where you're standing, look up at you with their weird and wide pleading eyes, mouthing sorry sentences. Lips like the legs of lab frogs on a slab, twitching sticky and staticky. Lifeless heads all the same.

It's said that if a rolling head rolls its way over to you, stops at your feet, that means you're obliged to scoop it up off the blackened ground, cradle it in the crook of your arm, and go find a body that's a good—or at least decent—fit for it. Peruse the shelves down at the service shops. It's a hell of a blessing to get found by a rolling head. A body joined, all oiled-up and slick as a slut, a layer of gauze between the worst asbestos winds and those pink parts that make you all too human.

Sometimes you see guys walking around the dust fields with their hands in their pockets, late night or early morning, kicking up dust, wandering around hoping to God a head will roll along and stop right there, right where they're standing. It's not so hard to imagine that sort of loneliness, is it?

The worms underground take everyone to the end of the line. I get on and wait. Sliding through the rooty and plugged webbing of the land. I get off and stop off at a water fountain. It's bone-dry.

This town is all circles; there's no such thing as sharp turns. There's nowhere to hang your coat. Not since the bedbugs started nesting in everything soft. They nest in the folds of facial tissue, festering in the pink plumbing of your neck—those loathsome bugs.

Outside beneath the horrible metal sky, I see a head rolling down the street. A dozen or so guys, they lunge for it, try to get in front of it, make the thing stop in front of their feet. But it doesn't stop. Just hops, flops around them with a spring-like intensity. I can't really blame them for trying, those guys. Just like I can't really blame the head for not wanting to stop for just any sad sack.

Dead-ends can be all kinds of awful if you come up against one and you don't know where you're going or where to turn to. I've spent too much time outside lately. I've sucked in too much dust. By now I've coughed up a bag of blood. Least I think it's blood. It could be tar.

Tonight on the television there's a program about sub-humanoid toddler creatures.

My refrigerator's filled-to-bursting with meat. I can't stop buying it. Ribs, T-bone steaks, ground chuck—it doesn't matter what it is.

The butcher, he doesn't have a name. You hardly hear the thunk, thunk, thunk of his cleavers ever since the cows and pigs and horses have gone missing. Can't say where they were trying to get to. Maybe drowned crossing the rivers or buried in the ash seas. It doesn't matter, really. What matters is that they're gone.

So I do my part. Chip in. I buy as much meat from him as I can afford and I stock it away. He'll keep his cleavers sharp a little longer, until things turn around. And I'll never forget the smell of something that lived as it turns—a reminder, really, for what's worming around beneath any sort of glow I might accidentally let myself feel on any given someday.

Carnivore

meat hanging on a hook
marbled fat serrated

hangnail of excess
terror body the hunger

grinding sluiced blood in
gutters burdened

a clock deep in
my eardrums

Negative Pressure

two bodies born
strange, housed in iron
lungs

on either side of a brick wall
the suck of negative pressure

an endless dumb
talk of black stars, of what it's
like to walk up walls

the twisted view
from the ceiling

Pinhead

My face is an abscess
Cut the cancer off my face
Put metal in me

Don't go into the basement
Crawlspace

Something is wrong
With the angles of the hallway
I don't want to die

I can't wait to die
I've always been here
In an explosion

As far as I know
It's been a terrible birthday party

The Nightmare Room

I cannot feel the walls they are like ghosts
in my remembering, tracing footprints
on my ceiling

skin shed and
bloodless broken bones
mended anew, angled awry—

I'll always remember
the shape of their teeth
the grind of their appetite

Their white masks
a disoriented clock
a ruined clock

Inside the Black Box

I have a bedroom somewhere
a mechanical island
where I sleep at night

There is a black box on my bed
and I am inside the black box

The black box is filled with invisible angles
    shifting
—like walking down a dark hallway of ever-
    changing faces

I cannot see my hand in front of my face
cannot fill the space inside the black box

I have stuffed my ears with handfuls of mouth
    slop

Don't try to block out the music of the man
    with his head on fire
you will have to deal with his anger—
and he can be so very angry

Don't turn down an invitation to the black
    church
you will be forced to wear a leash of hands
you will be forced to count the ticking of the
    black clock's hands

Untitled

In a house with no rooms a different house
a basement with no walls
a crawlspace with no end

In a town with no people a street
with no name, no houses
static wall of wet clay

In a house with no rooms a room with no
    windows
at the bottom: a staircase with no bottom
a hole leading to another hole

Another hole
there used to be a hole here
and now there is another hole

Cavity

Born of the same womb,
Some warped ovum

Twins in tissue, equal parts
blood and tonsil

A brother kind, lungs healthful
Arms malformed—a blue-faced horror—

The eater: wrangled freak
Black-cord monster

Mother husk, her dying
Wish for a total terror death

My Brother's Head

My brother's head was the shunned house
a blackened growth in the garden
in our neighbor's backyard

He'd speak, sometimes, then
my brother would. He'd sing the dirt song.

And together we'd
hide in the shade of those ivy-crawling
    shadows
faraway voices a blight
bird calls so unfamiliar

My Father's Head

My father's head turned inside-out,
lips pinned-back and teeth clenched,
mouth a newly disfigured dimension,

there, where the walls and the floor come
    together,
depending on the angle—forever vanishing

He taught me to hammer nails on their head,
to eye the craftsmanship in the darkness of the
    house,
to cherish shared blood, and all the weird light
we found there

My Family Grave

Their faces are long,
gaunt—
black holes for eyes—
and stretching

a stream, a screen
of smoke,
a silver projection
in the black sky

—precision
the arms of a music box—
the clicking metal parts
falling into place—

the sky is
starred with faces

the faces are the faces
of my family
a freshly
packed mound of dirt settling

a headstone
long smoothed over
by the weather

Ghost Factory

a lamb's skin draped over a fencepost
drying pink in the rays of the sun

a giant skull rotating in outer-space
eye sockets beaming acid light

it amazes me how I ever get to sleep at night

Chasm

Did you know about the cities
of fat swelling
in the ventricles of your heart?

Have I not told you
what's in that blood-soaked bag
at your feet?

There is a real disappointment
each time I let this old engine out,
tighten it, only to drop it down
a gear and hear the roar
deeper down somewhere
in the inferno

Death by a Thousand Cuts

Hey

Hatred's my steak
my heart's a muscle
and I've never once joked
about being
totally humorless

Please

Tell me, how far can you run?
I can do 15 miles without breaking
a sweat. Shithead
I'm serious
as Russian state-sponsored TV

Do you understand me?

You see this puddle of puke and shit?
I punched this right out
of some shithead's gut
I punched it right out—I thought about God
and I punched it the fuck right out

Humiliation

You see it in the eyes of the black cat perched
on the sill of a screened-in window tracking
such tight and unrecognizable sounds

And you remember: the worst place to be lost is
in the deep woods late at night; the worst place
to wait out a lightning storm is in a metal boat
in the center of a deep and dead lake

Say Kill, Kill, Kill

Scorched the ribbed roof of a horse's
Mouth on your insides, barbed, your blood
A soup, a tar-pit of cancer cells

Fashioned new bayonets for killing,
For the purity of aggression, for the widening
Of wounds and the freeing of fluids

A scraggly polar bear's muzzle worn raw,
Pinked and bloody, ulcerous bacteria eating
Away at the lining of his stomach

Moaning, "I can't stomach this
anymore. I don't have the stomach
for this hunger anymore."

Tyrant Unto Ruins

For years, the nameless blank letters were
addressed to the house on the street with the
swaying trees. A water tower in the distance,
neglected. A poisoned well

That house scraped inside-out, blackened by
flame—a million tiny crabs chipping away at
the stony seaside—the slow plinking of piano
lessons from the mythical blind boy's house

Our fear—those of us who remember—seeps
through open windows—a black fog—horror
fog—a maniac preacher cloaked on the street
corner—just listen to what he says

PART TWO

Coagulation of Holes

Chamber Music

Inside the glass building inside the glass
elevator shafting upward toward the light—
broken by devices prismatic, polygonal
obstructions—the dark creases of his facial
folds illumined, porous. His fingers
cantilevered over the bridge of his nose,
pinched eyes asquint, saying I can't deal with
the seething, not anymore, not like I used to.
Some shuffling of shoulders, the elevator doors
split, belling. Some rearrangement of bodies.
And then again. And again.

His night terrors are carefully designed, accurately angled, defined geometries. As he grows older, stunted, his once-twisting corridors of thought are blunted by a pressure, a hungry, sinkhole within. Darkened hallways compact to trapping cubes.

Frantic, reaching out into the nighttime, or pressing his fingers against the bathroom mirror, thinking you are inside a box; the box is so dark you do not know you are inside a box; the box is transparent and you do not know who is looking in. From beyond, he repeats the familiar formula.

The steepest vertigo pulses through his tangled guts.

Showering is a constant compulsion; scrubbing his skin red, dark drops of blood between his puckered toes, pinked by the tub water. Afterward, with the mirror steamed over, he feels a well of relief descend limitlessly, a reprieve from the tumor-bloom of the terror. His breathing, then, resembles a regular rhythm, a metronymic reminder to forgive all and any others he'd forearmed into the foggy distance.

In school, as a boy, he was shown a colorful chart, broken into parts, each integratively working together to demonstrate a single fact: the world holds 300 pounds of insects for every pound of human flesh.

The sunlight kills. Eats light, no reflection. Sweat builds greasy in the pink guttering of tear ducts.

An airplane overhead suddenly sprouts six legs, its belly hardening into overlapping plates, wings groaning upward, creasing, veining black through translucent tissue as they fold against the body. Its tail spasms a handful of lashes, shed, dropping off like a bomb, deadweight. Propeller drone hiccupping to a bowed harping, head angling narrow. Domed eyes bubble up, compressed with fractal webbing.

With a lightness so foreign, its new body bounds beyond the clouds, a spec in the sky, a black hole, and then nothing.

Inside Space

I hang a painting, and
when I look into the painting
—a painting of a room—

when I look into the room
I am in the room
inside the painting hanging

The room is filled with a hanged light
swinging from a string and
the light carves out the dimensions of the room

I struggle for the words as
my fingers struggle with the rope struggle
to get between the tightness

It is a horror this
—a disconnect—
I am unable to explain

The Abyss

There is nothing here.
A welling of memories. A mouthful
of ash. A handful of rotten pennies.
The chasm of the abyss.

A silhouette clouding a rectangle of light.
A staircase, swaying. A wall of unworn masks.
There is nothing beyond the window. There is
no one at the door.

Here is an exhibit of torture devices.
A man sitting in a dark room.
A dark room in a large and dark house.
Here is a man sitting in the dark.

Stranger

I have become a
stranger to myself

All darkness is
the same darkness—
autumnal

A highway unrolling into shadow
a city hidden within the back alleys of the city
undiscovered, feared

All mirrors are windows
All doors are walls

I have become a
monster, a pillager of misery,
interrogator of discomfort

All cancer is
the same cancer—
feeding on itself

A forgotten lighthouse
slick with tangled plants,
darkened by the mists of tidal crash

Every year, an identical news report is
broadcast within our homes:

It shows the same images, again and again:
the end of the winding pier, its slanted
    staircases swarmed
by millions of red-shelled crabs, a man—

his name and age are always the same—is
    invited into
the black waters below, disappeared

Every year, a reminder of the danger of storms
a reminder to build shrines, to link the fires
of superstition

All belief is
the same belief—
perpetual motion

Punching Clown

The man in the doctor mask places a single finger on my forehead, pushes hard, an I-need-an-elevator-right-now push, rocking me onto the balls of my feet. I am like one of those punching clowns, those inflatable things that just keeps standing up straight, keeps on taking the punches, rolling around a bit before somehow straightening. My heart is inflatable and filled to bursting with humiliation. My nose is swollen and red and irritated.

I try not to think about that time I ran that red light. I try not to think about the warbled and washed video footage they made me watch, of me behind the wheel of that car, running that red light and running into that little girl crossing the street—she was using the crosswalk, a red balloon in her hand. I remember, of course, as a matter of course. I remember how the balloon blipped up into the sky like it couldn't get away fast enough.

The man in the doctor mask removes that thing over the mask's mouth and smiles, shows me his teeth. I can see them there, through the mouth hole. I nod a bit, not out of affirmation, but because, instead, I'm still swiveling from the last stinging sock I took on the nose. I hate this man in the doctor mask. It is okay to hate some things. Some things leave you with no choice but to hate them. His teeth remind me of the toughness of things, of animals, of how everything alive is only fighting off hunger.

At this time of day, high noon, and on this kind of day, a lunar eclipse, the town square is almost entirely empty. Only I am there, in the town square. And the man in the doctor mask. The sky is like silver smoke trapped between two panes of curved glass: opaque and swirling. Any minute now and the wind will carry the stuttered clang of church bells. Any minute now and the square will fill with familiar faces. They will form a crowd, crowd in on one another, and wait. It will be the beginning.

I hear the caw of a crow, am barely able to turn and see that the wrought-iron fence lining the small hill near the cemetery is swarming with a murder of those terrible black birds. This does not bode well. The man in the doctor mask stands before me. Above me. A reminder. I do not hear the last noise. My words do not make the sounds I so desperately wish I could make them make. My last thoughts are of the red balloon, are with the red balloon, floating upward and into those surely heavenly heavens.

The Destruction Loops

1-8

I've let my blood out in a steamy bath
I've jammed a butter knife into the toaster
Lied down on my back and dropped a shot put
    on my face
I stuffed balls of newspaper print in my mouth
And spelled the state capitals in alphabetical
    order

I allowed myself to be hypnotized at the count
    of 8
The snap of my neck the snap of a hypnotist's
    fingers
The hypnotist showed me the earth as the
    angels see it
The streets are a twisted maze and we are lost
    in the maze
We are born walking into the world's maze

At the count of 4 you will forget your confusion
The bathroom is filled with steam and the
    mirrors are steamed over
You cannot see yourself or your face in the
    mirror
The maze is all right angles
You are born into a confusion of angles
You will realize your confusion at the count of
    4

1 – turn right
2 – turn right again
3 – turn right again
4 – turn right again

You are where you began
You must make this circuit twice
You are no longer lost in this section of the
    maze

I hear the snap of fingers the snap of my neck
I am alone in a great square in a gray city
There are clouds adrift in the swollen sky
The clouds are swollen with acid rain
The gray city is one of many on an island in the
    ocean
The ocean is green
Its green waters are a bath of acid eating away
    at the coastline

You cannot see yourself in the mirror
Soon the clouds will open up and let loose
    their rains
You will strip naked and let them eat away at
    your skin
In the morning your skeleton will be found by a
    group of hungry lions
The lions will have ribs like wishbones
    pushing out at their fur
And they will pick you clean
You have given them a fullness
The meat on your bones will have completed
    its circuit
You will feel that you have done the right thing

You will feel an angel place a heavy hand on
    your shoulder
You will close your eyes and count to 8

You are clean now
You have smeared jam on your toast
You are no longer hungry
It is warm here in the lion's den

9-11

The bomb is just a mortar shell connected to a
    blasting cap
Connected to some wires connected to a
    wireless phone
Stuffed inside the rotting gut of a dead dog
Hidden in a trash heap

Our lungs are just hollow organs connected to
    some other hidden stuff
And I read once that the weight of the ocean
    will eventually crush
All of the oxygen out of the water

And I wonder what new darkness the giant
    cephalopods will disappear into

The overpressure of an explosion can tear a
    hole in the space between things
And pull a body inside its hidden folds
Squid tentacles will reach up from the black
    depths of the ocean
And pull down ships filled with frantic men
    who still believe in the frightful myths of
    monsters

12-35

With the right numbers we have learned how
    much bricks weigh
We have learned to always build bricks the
    same shape
How to stack them
How to make a load-bearing wall
The crux of a keystone

The floor of our new home is covered in the
    metal shavings of freshly cut keys
The sunlight is filled with floating golden
    spirals
It is an enterprise to take apart what we build
Recursively dividing our original structure

Your jealous lover paid a young boy to throw
    acid in your face
Your face has long been disfigured by acid
I cannot remember the build of your face

How did the pieces of your face fit together

There are walls between us
I am forgotten inside this place
I am a forgotten dead body bricked-in in a dark
    room
I am breathing dust

Your bones are made of dust
You always wore the same perfume
It was the smell of light at the bottom of a pool

There is chlorine in my eyes
I cannot see the inside of this place

My thoughts are caught in an endless loop
I put a gun to my head and shoot myself in the
    head
The gun is an endless revolver
The bullet skirts my skull
The bullet pings against the brick wall
I am bleeding on the floor
There are golden spirals here on the floor

I am lost inside the spiraling shell of a giant
    and very dead snail
I say to the snail
Let's build our home together and let's live in
    our home together

36-59 (partially destroyed)

Fragment #1:

That old video screen has become the retina of
    the mind's eye
And the eye is the image accumulator
The eye is floating in outer space
The outer space of the skull is trapped light
The eye sees light and takes in light and is
    filled with light
The eye is rotating in outer space
Wrapped in a webby vortex of veins
Twirling down time's narrowing cone
A grid of green light
The black pool stretching your face into a
    stream of sound
The video screen is receiving your
    transmissions
The video screen is pushing outward into the
    room
Enveloping your family
Can you see the sound
Can you hear the volume of the vortex

Fragment #2:

We have triangulated our signals
Searched out the shortest distance
And heard our names echoing back to us
From inside the swirl of a black hole
The drift of two lonely satellites
Passing by
Gliding over the planet's blue-glow haze
Lasers flicking in the darkness
A plasticky clicking in the great silence
Silk strands of white light
The earth is spinning surrounded by its lonely
    satellites
Forever revolutions in a slow orbit
Hatchlings tethered to their core
There is no such thing as distance

Fragment #3:

We are receiving transmissions from oblivion
The black pools at the bottom of the narrowing cone
The reality of the video screen has become our reality
It is a new reality
We are awake and we are hungry
We are eating light
Our eyes are filled with light
They are swarmed with swollen veins
Aligned on a vector
The veins pulse with a new light
The transmissions enter us
A laser beam burns a hole between our eyes
We have been gifted our memory
We have been gifted a new memory
There is a hole in our forehead
The edge of space has broadened beyond
Time is balanced on a broadened beam
And we move along the green lines of a great vector
Always skirting the empty black spaces
Always searching out the shortest distance
We drilled a hole through our flesh and our bone
We bled into our eyes
Our eyes are swimming in pools of blood

60-90

I am driving my car
I stop at red lights
I drive through green lights
If the light is yellow I will accelerate

My car goes 0-60 in no time
There is a yellow light
I make a decision
I drive through a yellow light—accelerate

I see a car with a brick on its gas pedal
I see a car accelerating into a brick wall
I see a burst of flames and smoke

The car is driving
No one is in control of the car
There is a brick wall
It will always happen the same way
There will always be a burst of flames and
    smoke

I am in the driver's seat
I am going through the yellow light
My body is safe inside the walls of its privilege
I am privileged to understand the universe

I remember a scene from a movie
I remember a burst of flames and smoke
I can see a car slamming into a brick wall
The car is always running into the brick wall

Out in the universe there is a very large human
    skull
Its eye sockets fill with intermittent moonlight
As it revolves in its orbit

Its empty space filled with images of safety and
    privilege
There is a man inside the human skull

The outer space of the skull is trapped light

There is a man in the driver's seat
He stops at red lights
He drives through green lights
He sees a car
He is alone in the universe
He sees what might be a car

91 – 99

I fell asleep when I was sleeping and I woke up in someone else's dream

His thoughts were just like mine
He lived in the terrible house with laughing windows

He was still inside his mother
His mother wore a thin nightgown and stood at the top of the stairs
I saw her there—in the motherland—in the moonlight

She spoke the soft pink language
Her face was torn and her feet were not there
Before he was born

His mother ran her hands over her pregnant belly
—the Motherland—
She saw a dead body and it was her body
The only dead body she had ever seen was her own

She has bleach inside a black box
inside her belly
It is her worst kind of comfort

She asks herself:

what is the worst
that could happen—

if I set myself on fire?

would it be worse if I died
or did not die?

seashell skin,
smooth and pink,
unrecognizable

is what I really want
to be unrecognizable?

or to melt

the frosted ground
of the winter cornfield
a light, ablaze—
a beacon in the dark

a signal to be put out

-

I am so very tired
I will never sleep again
I will never wake up again

∞

You begin in the black box,
in the darkness,
and it is wholly possible that
there are no walls
around you

You begin
in the darkness of
the black box around you,
and it is wholly possible that
You begin

around you
there are no walls—
in the darkness,
in the black box,
and it is wholly possible, that

Pluto

Then finally there was the day when the whole world beyond his bedroom window appeared to be engulfed in the acid light

He wanted to go over to his neighbor's house but he could not go outside because everything outside appeared to be engulfed in the acid light

He stayed in bed and watched a VHS tape

He was still young and would never know the slow grind of his body breaking down and for this he was relieved

The TV screen showed an image of a man in black robes turning over itself in a loop overexposed into some sort of oblivion

Death Manual: Instructions for Participation in Mass Suicide Ritual

The difference between 1/3 and 1/4 is only 1, if you're considering the number 12. If you're considering the number 24, the difference doubles to 2. This is the difference.

You are born out of a fire with these instructions written on a crumpled piece of paper stuffed inside of your mouth. You are born as a skeleton with bones on fire and eyes filled with the acid of light.

Bathe in the light and know the touch of God. Flunk. You will die in the fire, on trial, and harangued by masses of the cloaked, the incensed, brothers-in-arms and blind, unworldly meat eaters.

Every time an angel dies a serial killer is born in the cement confines of a dark mansion. Do not fear him. You will forget everything you have ever thought of as impossible. A desiccated husk—once dreamt.

Exoskeletal memory: in the event, remove the skin from your fingertips, immolate your face, remove your teeth with pliers. The core of the planet is black blood. Sockets ratchet—meat grind.

You will receive these instructions in the form of a letter, in the form of a communication. Allow invitation when recognized. Discard manual beforehand, by swallowing, by the fire's consumption.

Below the Violet

The brothers were born within mere minutes of one another, the first arriving in the caul, slicked. His skin looked chewed by the rasping light. His lungs opened up healthy and his cries were like something wholly wild, an animal in buck. The second brother discharged cleanly, quietly. He would be the amenable one, no doubt. Their mother smiled at this then flattened, eyelids fluttering, thoughts lost in gnawing dream. The nurses and the doctor did what they could but she slipped beyond their reach, face still masked with labor sweat. Her body was zippered into a formless black bag, disappeared down into the morgue. Her bed was made available for another.

The brothers, blanket-bundled, were set carefully behind glass in the maternity ward. Then the focus shifted to administration. Where were the mother's papers? Anyone waiting for her in the waiting room? Who would be notified of her passing? Who was the father and where had he gone? No one had any answers. No one at the hospital remembered admitting her. The grainy and over-scanned security footage showed no record of her having come through the ER, or any other entrance for that matter. Had she ever said anything during labor? Mentioned her name? Had anyone asked for her name? No one could remember. The facts went slippery under scrutiny. Every inquiry dulled lifeless.

Outside the hospital, the sun was high and white. In a few hours the moon took its place.

As directed, an orderly conceded his way into the morgue, startled himself on the catch of the gurney's metal tracks. His simple hands unzipped the black bag the mother's body had been put inside but her body was no longer there. The bag was empty, dry. The orderly forgot why he'd gone cold in that room or what he was searching for. He looked in the bag again, angled its ruffled emptiness in the light, hoping to remind himself of who he was, what he was doing, and uncovered a hole. He heard a sound rise from within the hole, a strike from deep down, something familiar but not quite—his mother's voice. He climbed onto the gurney and into the hole and curtained the bag shut behind him, forgotten.

A house painted gray too long ago stood abandoned, surrounded by other houses of similarly earnest design, the eaves of its upstairs windows licked black by the memory of rolling flames. That house was filled with items of convenience, a metal device to remove walnuts from their shells. Some streets removed, an identical house painted gray more recently would no doubt be filled with precisely those same items, whole shelves and drawers of chrome gleam, the swirled grain of wood polished reflective. In the early summer evenings, lace curtains hung over open windows warm in the sun, the whole room a pinked lung sighing unbearably in the west winds.

From the sky, the roads of the town surrounding the hospital resembled the web of a spider with uneven pairings of legs, a system of connections spun tilted from a center in tight angles. Whole streets had been eaten away, the broken bodies of trees rooted to plunging walls of soil.

PART THREE

Evaporation

Screwhead

wrapping organs around VHS heads,
disassembled and boxed, shoveled into the fire,
little green men living in hexagonal
communities

retinal detachment, recorded onto twisted tape,
exposed, a dead place in a different time zone

the shoe bombers, the cloud grazers,
wunderkinds, covered in gasoline,
uncontrollable vomiting, a free trip to the
vacation resort under

the hole in the sky

bleach

heart of husks, car parts, the pull and the
spasm, the contractions

I have gigantic titanium hands, I can cup the
earth with a single hand, a neon blue fiberglass
chew toy, flakes of dead information

alien stomach sack burns a blue spark,
survived the death house and grew up and old

the hushed wilderness at time of sleep: the red
river a gush of negative, of light flood, bug
chirps and the acid crush of atomic bloom

there will always be a market for yachts,
regurgitating worms to children, black forests
of eyeless fish

razor-blade walls meet in sharp corners, the
sting of an airplane passing overhead, the dusty
sky a rattling telephone

a boy sees an ant on his foot and bursts into
flames, clock tower chimes: time to die. the
neighbors all saying

to one another he's doing it again he's doing it
again it's so disgusting. invincible plastic cup.
clown suit. unscrewing all the screws, writing
instruction manuals for new bombs

laminated asthma

pass the naked fat child piddling asquat in a
puddle of gasoline, webbed fingers waving, a
chub

dropout, high on hate and the shush of
highway

austerity, she said, the sterile churches of
childhood and the boner wood benches of
toolsheds

steel wires beneath my fingernails, picking
black buzzard meat from between the child's
teeth

nightmarish exoskeleton shelled like a subway
car, pouring black through the chimney flue,
bristling, the walls black from abuse

hatching, a battery-powered ball-peen hammer

intestinal tract of half-digested paste, yearbook
pinhead slugs eyes scratched out

fathers, uncles, brothers, nephews, sons—
everyone executed, electrocuted

austerity, she said, and held tight my hand

anthemic power violence

vacuum continuum of ruined lives like lead
dust drifting over the river, the perfumey
glittering gleam of its wombing bloom

scraping the cleaver over the crib, he says

austerity, she said, a fog voice, sitting naked in
barren rooms, whacking wasps out of the
breeze

dug worms from dirt, molasses of swimming
guts

trekking backward through the woods at night,
her and I, our bluster of breath, back down to
the snowcapped thighs of thunderous gods

look at the ground below

and you will find an endless hole

where once there was none

look at the ground below

and you will find an endless hole

where once there was none

look at the ground below

and you will find an endless hole

where once there was none

look at the ground below

and you will find an endless hole

where once there was none

look at the ground below

and you will find an endless hole

where once there was none

look at the ground below

and you will find an endless hole

where once there was none

look at the ground below

and you will find an endless hole

where once there was none

look at the ground below

Acknowledgements

Infinite gratitude to the editors of the following journals who published some of these pieces, often in morphed or masked forms: *Action Yes*, *LIES/ISLE*, *Everyday Genius*, *Radioactive Moat*, *Mud Luscious*, *Broken Toujours*, *The Scrambler*, and *JMWW*.

"My Brother's Head" was originally published by Mud Luscious Press as part of the Stamp Stories Project.

"The Destruction Loops" was originally published as a limited-edition chapbook by Solar Luxuriance.

gnOme is a secret press specializing in the publication of anonymous, pseudepigraphical, and apocryphal works from the past, present, and future.

"I am halfway between these appearances and that which invalidates them, *that* which has neither name nor content, *that* which is nothing and everything" (Michel).

gnOme is acephalic. All profits from print sales go to the authors.

www.ingramcontent.com/pod-product-compliance
Lightning Source LLC
Chambersburg PA
CBHW031458040426
42444CB00007B/1138